Contents

W9-BKF-483

Build it!
There are plenty of ideas for epic builds as you charge through this book.

Play it!
Look out for these great ideas for minifigure action. Create castle adventures of your own!

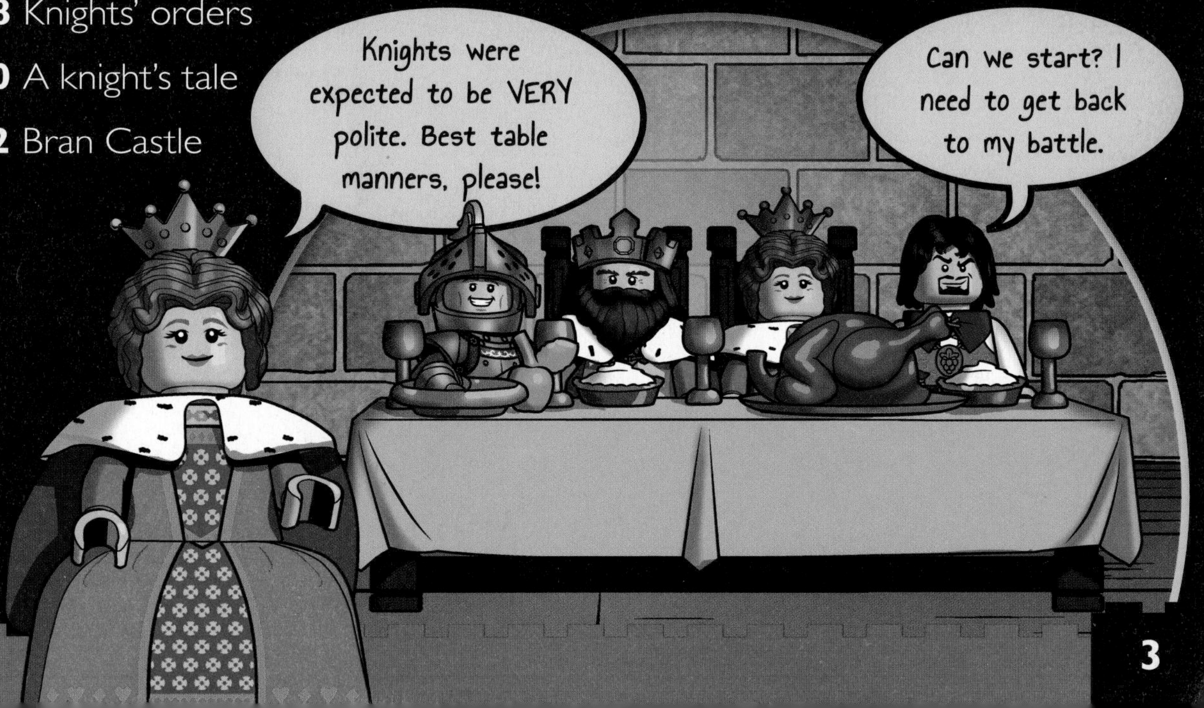
Knights were expected to be VERY polite. Best table manners, please!
Can we start? I need to get back to my battle.

Medieval times

It's about 800 years ago in Europe. Kings and queens rule many lands. A ruler's most loyal subjects, his lords and ladies, live in towering castles and have armies of brave knights.

KNIGHT FACTS
Look out for these shields in the book. They have extra facts about knights and castles.

Woo-hoo! It's taken me 14 years to become a knight. I'm off to win a battle! No time for tea, lads!
Good luck! We'll keep the castle safe.

It took me an hour to get my suit of armor on!
Knights have all the fun. We serfs get to do the really hard work. Siiigh.
Hey, knight! I challenge you to a battle. And if you are a real knight, you can't say no!

Castles through time

The first castles were built about 1,000 years ago. For the next 500 years, amazing castles were built all over Europe and western Asia. As time went on, castles got bigger and tougher.

Motte and bailey

The first castles were wooden towers on hills, called mottes. Each motte had a fenced yard around it, called a bailey.

Stone castles

Wooden castles could easily catch fire, so stone castles were built next. The walls were very thick.

THE KEEP

The tower in the center of a castle is called a keep.

The queen of England lives in Windsor Castle. It's the oldest castle in Europe that people still live in.
These motte-and-bailey castles are great! They take just weeks to build.

Stone castle walls were 5 to 30 feet (1.5 to 9 m) thick and often 40 feet (12.2 m) high. This is going to be a tough climb!

The castle fortress

As castles grew bigger, they needed more workers. Soon, castles were like mini-towns.

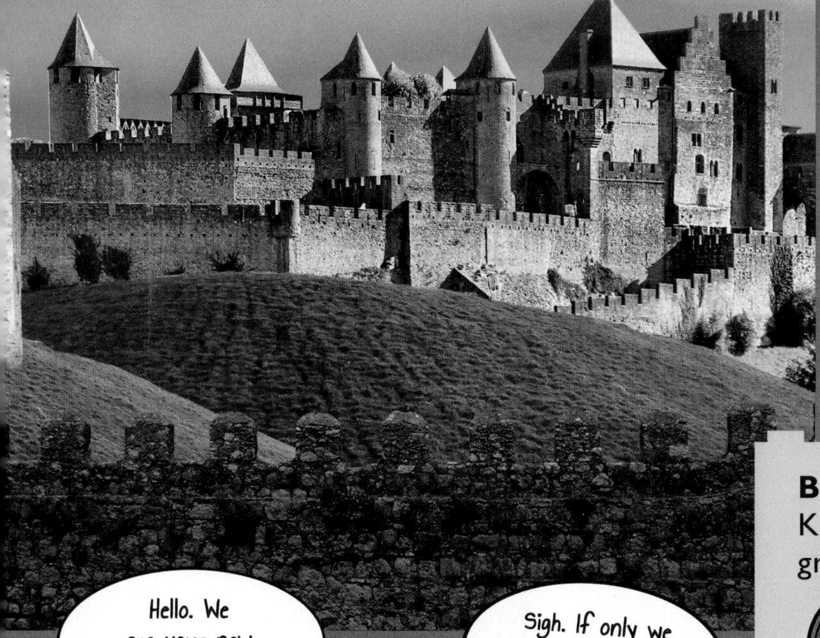

Build it!

The enemy is on its way! Build a strong castle. Here are some features to help you.

Tower

High wall

Battlement

Drawbridge

Window

Flag

Build it bigger!

Kings and queens had the greatest castles of all. They were centers of power in their lands. Build a king his strongest-ever castle.

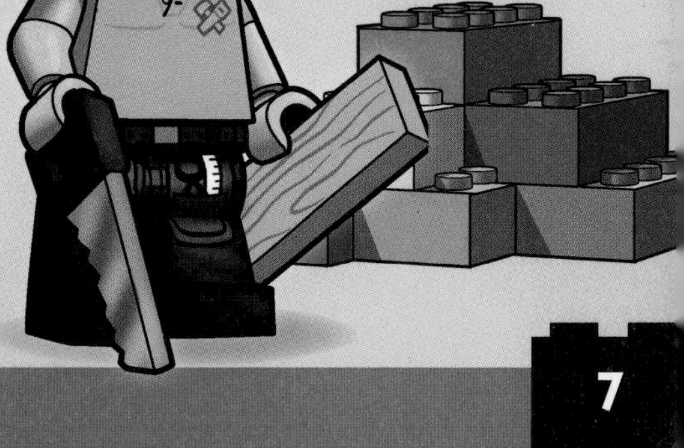

Hello. We are your new neighbors. Grrrr.
Sigh. If only we had a castle made of stone, like me.

Lord of the castle

Medieval kings and queens had to keep control of far-off lands. They gave their favorite lords lands to build castles on. All the people in and around a castle worked for the lord, not themselves.

I'm in charge. I make sure that my army of knights is strong and everyone is working hard.
No, I'm in charge. I run things day to day.

Lord and lady

The lord and lady were in charge of everybody who lived and worked in the castle.

FIGHT FOR ME!

A king might give land for a castle if a lord helped him in war.

I protect the lord and his castle when it's under attack. Grrrr.
Everyone's always hungry! I cook the food that comes from the fields. Where's the serf?
I think I've found the surf, dude!
She said "SERF," not "SURF"!

Knights
Knights were the most important soldiers. They rode horses.

Workers
A castle was a small town. Soldiers, blacksmiths, cooks, and servants all lived there.

Serfs
Serfs were poor people who worked on the land. They farmed food for the castle.

Knight school

KNIGHT FACT
There are still knights in the United Kingdom. This is one of the highest honors a person can achieve.

Most knights were from noble families, the sons of lords or other knights. They started their training as children, and trained for 14 years to be the best!

The page

At age 7, a nobleman's son became a page. A page learned about hunting, armor, weapons, and good manners.

The squire

At 14, a page became a squire. A squire worked for a knight. He armed the knight for battle and learned how to be a strong, brave fighter.

I'm not sure this knight thing is right for me . . . I'm getting cold feet.
Now I'm going to give you a knock so that you remember the rules.
Ouch! What was I supposed to remember?

Arise, sir knight!

The next day, the squire was dubbed. His lord knocked him on his shoulder with a sword. Now he was a real knight.

Almost a knight

At 21, the squire became a knight. The evening before, he was given a freezing-cold bath. He then prayed, all night.

KNIGHT'S PRIZE

The knight was given a sword and shield the day he was knighted.

The knight's code

A knight wasn't expected just to be a good fighter. He also had to behave very well and prove that he was extremely brave. He had to follow the knight's code.

The code of honor
A knight had to be chivalrous. That meant being polite, loyal, and brave. If a knight was challenged to a fight, he had to accept. He had to show courage.

True love
Knights LOVED the idea of being in love. They wrote love poems and tried to impress ladies with their bravery. A knight often jousted to win a lady's heart.

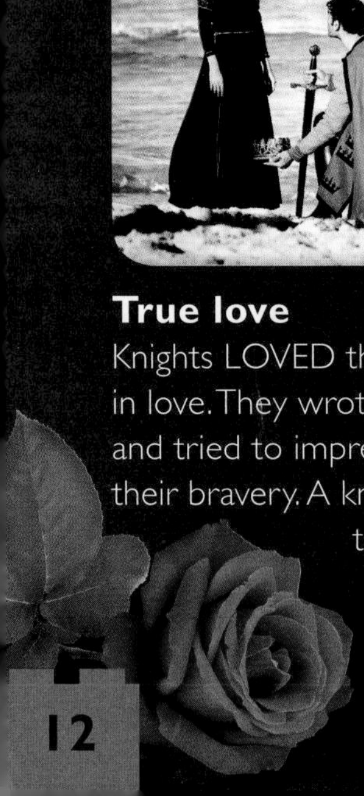

A knight's code of dos and don'ts

What beautiful hair you have.
Yikes! I'm out of here . . . !
Hmm. That outfit is foul (fowl, get it?!)
Pardon me!
I'm ready for you . . . grrrr!
You won, fair and square!

DO be polite at all times.

DON'T hug a lady in public.

DO tell the truth.

DON'T be rude.

DO fight with courage.

DON'T cheat.

Rules to become a knight!

Telling tales

Minstrels were poets and musicians. They traveled around, telling stories of brave knights. Many of these stories were then written down.

The joust

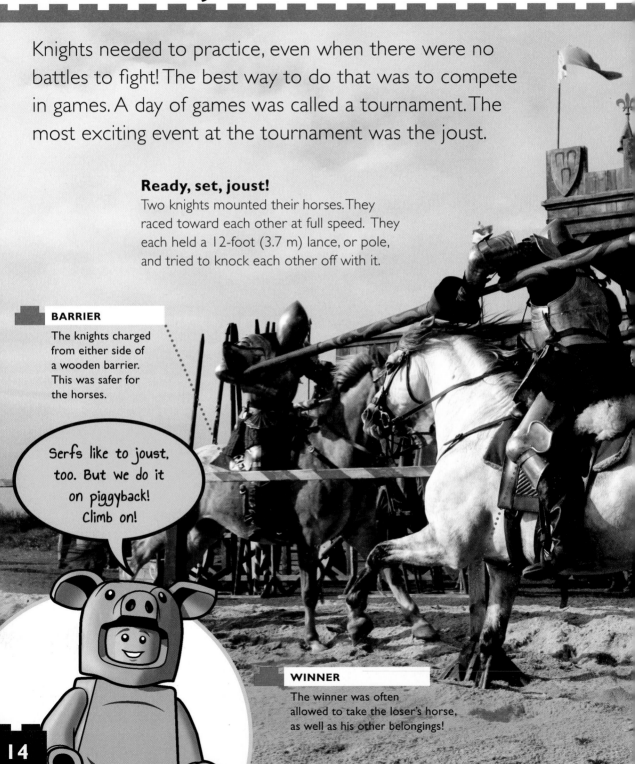

Knights needed to practice, even when there were no battles to fight! The best way to do that was to compete in games. A day of games was called a tournament. The most exciting event at the tournament was the joust.

Ready, set, joust!

Two knights mounted their horses. They raced toward each other at full speed. They each held a 12-foot (3.7 m) lance, or pole, and tried to knock each other off with it.

BARRIER

The knights charged from either side of a wooden barrier. This was safer for the horses.

Serfs like to joust, too. But we do it on piggyback! Climb on!

WINNER

The winner was often allowed to take the loser's horse, as well as his other belongings!

Build it!
Build a tournament area for your jousting knights!

CHEERING CROWDS

Crowds cheered for their favorite knights to win the contest.

STANDS

Huge stands were specially built for tournaments.

Watch out!

Jousting knights were told to be careful not to really hurt each other.

Hey, evil knight. I have defeated you. Now I can take your horse, your weapons, and your evil helmet . . .
That's fine. Take it all, except for the helmet. I LOVE my evil helmet . . .

A knight's tale

The legend of

KING ARTHUR'S ROUND TABLE

King Arthur's knights argued about who was the most important. King Arthur made them a round table so that everyone was equal.

PLAY IT!
Find out about the stories of King Arthur's knights. What amazing adventures will your knights have?

A legend is a story that is sometimes based on true events. In a famous legend, King Arthur was said to be king of England about 1,500 years ago. Many people didn't want him to be king, and attacked his kingdom. Luckily for Arthur, he had a wizard named Merlin to help him. He also had a magic sword called Excalibur, which defeated all enemies. Arthur chose 24 of his favorite, bravest knights to live and work with him at his castle, Camelot. The knights made up lots of rules that told them how to behave. These rules became the code of chivalry that all knights had to live by.

In legend, King Arthur pulled a sword from a stone to become king.
Yes, the sword could be pulled only by the rightful king of England.
Hmm, that gives me an evil idea. All I need is a sword and some strong glue . . .

Play it! Here are some ideas . . .

1 *Do your knights argue, or are they friends?*

2 *Is there a wizard in your knight world?*

3 *Who is your most evil knight?*

Into battle

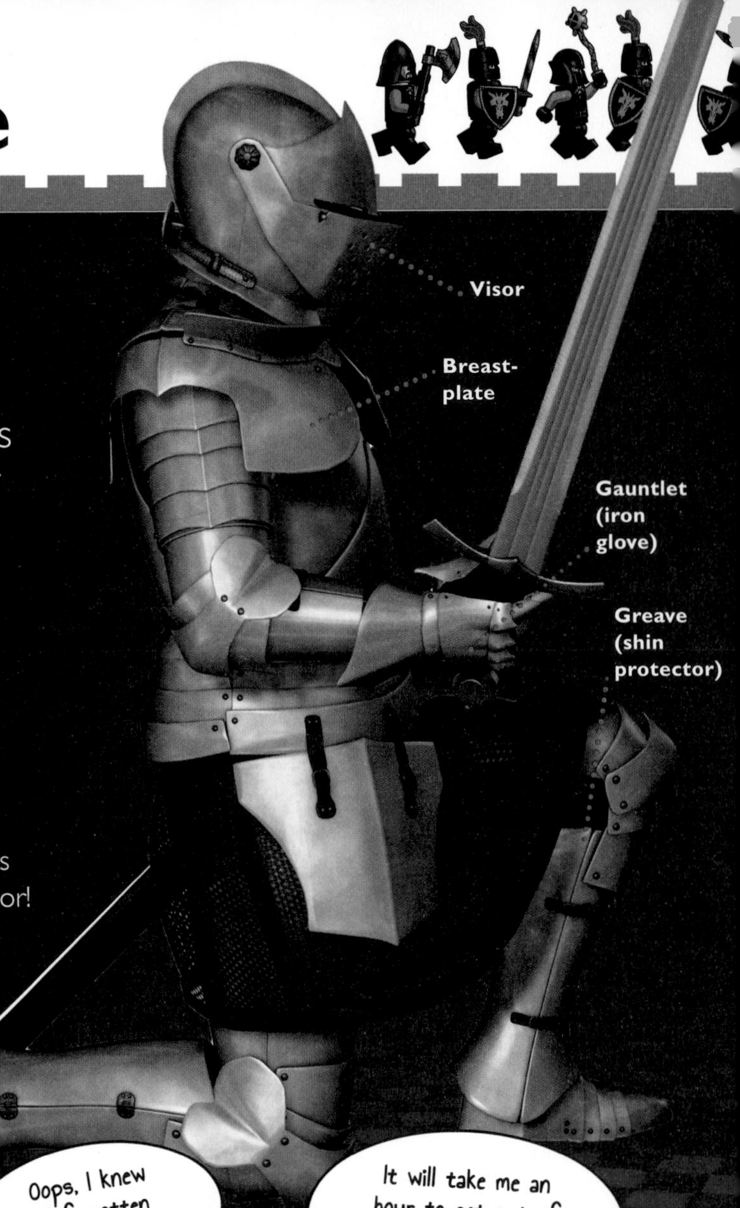

Visor
Breast-plate
Gauntlet (iron glove)
Greave (shin protector)

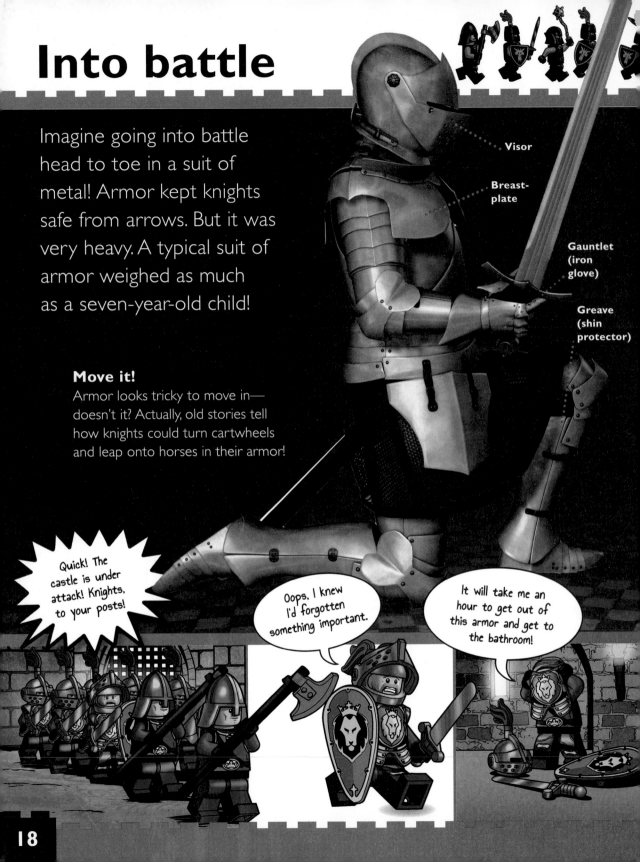

Imagine going into battle head to toe in a suit of metal! Armor kept knights safe from arrows. But it was very heavy. A typical suit of armor weighed as much as a seven-year-old child!

Move it!
Armor looks tricky to move in—doesn't it? Actually, old stories tell how knights could turn cartwheels and leap onto horses in their armor!

Quick! The castle is under attack! Knights, to your posts!
Oops, I knew I'd forgotten something important.
It will take me an hour to get out of this armor and get to the bathroom!

Chain mail

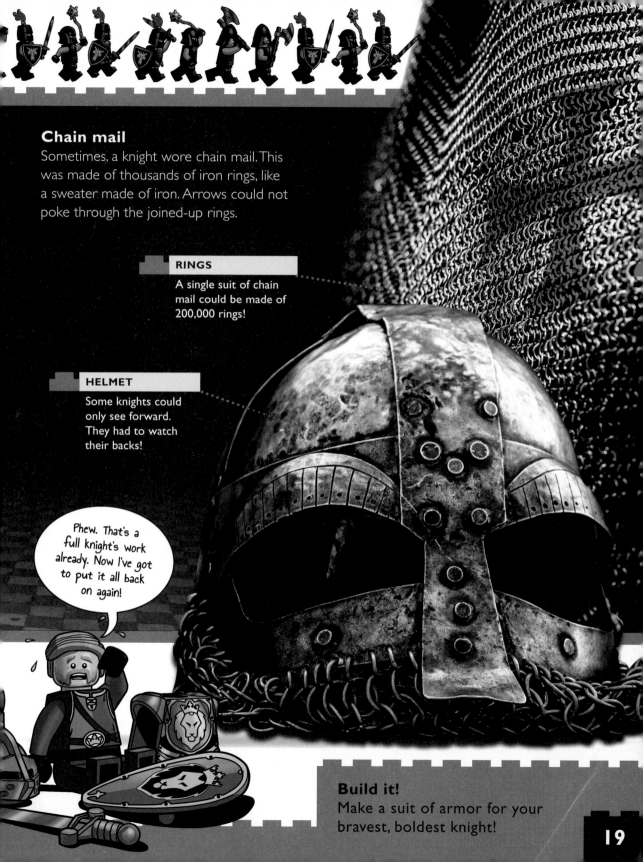

Sometimes, a knight wore chain mail. This was made of thousands of iron rings, like a sweater made of iron. Arrows could not poke through the joined-up rings.

RINGS

A single suit of chain mail could be made of 200,000 rings!

HELMET

Some knights could only see forward. They had to watch their backs!

Phew. That's a full knight's work already. Now I've got to put it all back on again!

Build it!

Make a suit of armor for your bravest, boldest knight!

The warhorse

Knights were the only soldiers who rode horses on the battlefield. The warhorse was the most important horse a knight ever owned. It was powerful and speedy.

Horse armor

In battle, a knight depended on his horse. It had to be strong enough to carry him and brave, too. Knights put armor on their horses to protect them.

I trained this horse to kick and bite, like you told me to . . .
Excellent! Just what I need on the battlefield. Hold it still, squire!
Ouch! I'm off!

Build it!
Build an arena to train your warhorses.

HEAD ARMOR
A warhorse had head armor that was called a chamfron.
SADDLE
The saddle had a high back and front to keep the knight balanced when he fought.
LEG COMMANDS
The knight would tell the horse what to do just by using his legs. His hands held his weapons.

A knight's tale The legend of

GEORGE AND THE DRAGON

Stories of St. George spread all over Europe, and he became a saint in many countries.

PLAY IT!
Can you invent a brave knight of your own? Where does the knight go and who does the knight rescue?

St. George, who slayed a dragon and saved a princess

Once upon a time, there was a brave knight named George. He traveled by horse across many lands. One day, he met a man who told him that a dragon was attacking his village. The villagers gave the dragon all their food, animals, and treasures. But the dragon did not stop. The king's knights could not defeat it. So the king gave his only daughter to the dragon. When George heard this, he rode straight to the dragon, which was about to gobble up the princess. George attacked and defeated it. He saved the village and the princess.

People once thought that dinosaur bones were from dragons.
Hmm. Are you sure that dragons don't exist?
Hold your fire! Stand back, knight. I've got this under control.

Play it! Here are some ideas . . .

1. *Give your knight a brave name.*
2. *Does your knight meet dragons or princesses?*
3. *Whom does your knight rescue?*

Coats of arms

I'm looking out for this shield. It belongs to Richard I, king of England. Go, king, go!
No, king, no! I'm cheering for the other side.

To battle! When all the knights were in full armor on a battlefield, it was tricky to tell who was who! Knights decorated themselves and their horses so that everyone knew who they were.

Coat of arms
Each knight chose a colorful design, called a coat of arms. This shield shows a royal coat of arms. Everyone knew that it belonged to the king.

Banners

Many knights and lords carried banners with their coats of arms onto the battlefield. Their soldiers could easily find them.

The herald

On the battlefield, heralds carried messages between knights and commanders. Heralds also announced knights at jousts.

HERALDRY

Heralds had to be great at recognizing coats of arms. Today the study of coats of arms is known as heraldry.

Build it!

Build a shield with your own coat of arms. Knights often used these designs.

Fish

Lion

Bull

Fleur-de-lis

Unicorn

Rooster

Eagle

Rose

Build it bigger!

Now that you've designed one coat of arms, design a whole battlefield of shields! Use lots of different colors and patterns.

One of the most important battles won by knights was the Battle of Hastings in 1066.

TAPESTRY

The Bayeux Tapestry, made at the time, shows scenes from the battle.

There was no internet in Medieval times! We know what things looked like through art.

A Medieval painting of a battle

I have to mix my own paint! Elderberries make a great purple color.
Red paint comes from red dirt.

Look at the tapestry! The knights are fighting on horseback with long spears. We foot soldiers used bows and arrows.

Battle of Hastings

This battle was between the Anglo-Saxon English and a Norman invading army. The Normans won and their leader, William, became King of England.

LONG STORY

The tapestry is 231 feet (70 m) long.

A stone carving of a jousting knight

Keep still. It takes a month to make a carving.
What do I look like? What do I look like?
It's a Sir Prize!

Knights' orders

KNIGHT FACT
The Order of St. John still exists today, based on the original order. The people in it look after sick people in emergencies.

From about 1100, many knights across Europe invented orders. Members had to follow rules and do the jobs that were given to them.

Is this the Order of St. John tent? I've walked 2,000 miles (3,220 km) and have really sore feet.
Oh, I see. You've got your boots on the wrong feet.

Teutonic knight

Order of St. John

Knights might be badly hurt in battle. The knights of the Order of St. John set up hospitals to help them.

Build it!
Build a hospital for the Order of St. John to work in.

Teutonic Order
This was an order of German knghts. Their motto was "Help, Defend, Heal."

Order badges
Each knightly order had a special badge, which knights wore around their necks. This is the badge of the Order of the Golden Fleece.

In 1457, Danish knights started the Order of the Elephant. No one knows why they chose elephants. Their necklace, with elephants and towers, is still worn today.
But these are the only feet I've got!
Arrgh! What is that?!

A knight's tale

EDWARD THE BLACK PRINCE

Edward never became king of England, because he died while his father was still on the throne.

PLAY IT!
Knights started their own orders when they didn't get in to the Order of the Garter. The Order of the Stoat and the Ear and the Order of the Bath really existed. Invent your own order.

Edward the Black Prince

In medieval times, there was a prince of England named Edward. He was known as the Black Prince because he wore a black tunic and carried a black shield. He won many battles in France and Spain and was a very brave knight. He even captured the king of France and held him prisoner for many years. The Black Prince's father, Edward III, started the Order of the Garter. The king and prince were members, and they chose 24 others to join them. It was considered the most important order of the time, and it still exists in England today.

Edward left me out! I'm starting a new club. The Order of the Bravest and Most Handsome Knights in the World . . . Ever.
You can't make it up. You have to do something brave . . .
I'll do something brave. I'll rescue you from that enormous hat . . .

Play it! Here are some ideas . . .

1 *What is your order called?*

2 *How many knights can join it?*

3 *Does it have a badge?*

A well in the middle of the castle is 187 feet (57 m) deep. That's like digging down the height of an 18-story building!

Bran Castle

In 1212, the Teutonic knights built a wooden castle called Bran Castle in Transylvania (today's Romania). They built it on a high hilltop in between two mountain ranges. This area was used as a road between Europe and Asia, and the castle protected Transylvania from invaders. The castle was rebuilt in stone in 1377. In 1927, hidden passageways were discovered in the castle. A staircase hidden behind a fireplace runs from the first floor to the third floor. Who knows why it was put there! Bran Castle is nicknamed Dracula's Castle after the vampire made famous in Bram Stoker's story. Although Stoker never visited it, the castle is now a museum.

Hmm, there's something spooky about this castle.
That might be because Bran Castle is supposed to be where Dracula lived.
Now you tell me . . .
Are you the pizza guy? No garlic bread!
We vampire bats have a lot in common with that Dracula dude. He's fang-tastic!

Castle defense

The castle was the center of power in the land. If an enemy wanted the power, it had to take the castle. Every part of the castle was built to defend it against an enemy.

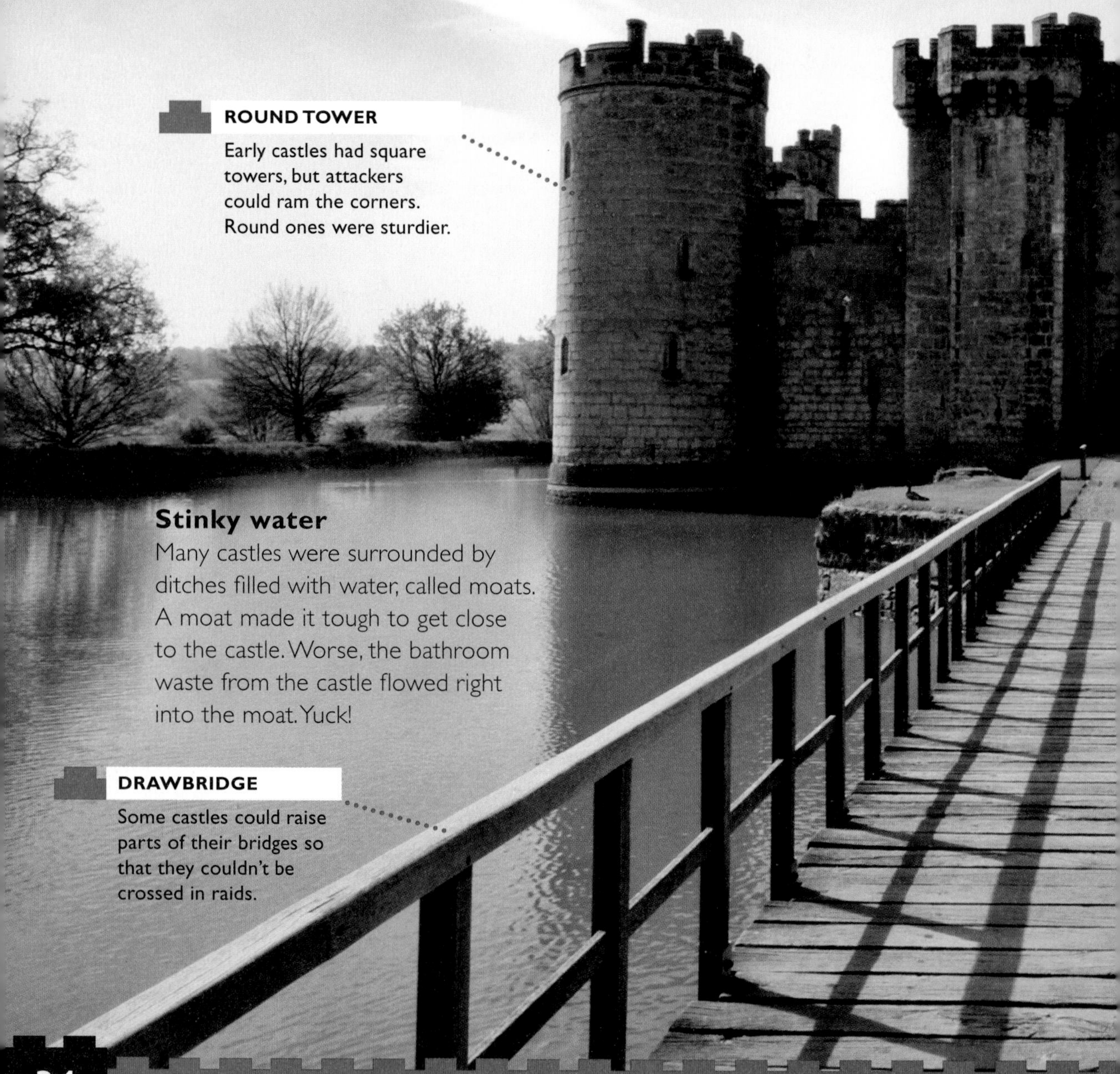

ROUND TOWER

Early castles had square towers, but attackers could ram the corners. Round ones were sturdier.

Stinky water

Many castles were surrounded by ditches filled with water, called moats. A moat made it tough to get close to the castle. Worse, the bathroom waste from the castle flowed right into the moat. Yuck!

DRAWBRIDGE

Some castles could raise parts of their bridges so that they couldn't be crossed in raids.

Build it!
Build a wide moat around a castle that no one can swim across.

BATTLEMENT
Archers could hide behind the tall, teethlike bricks and fire through the gaps.
ARROW SLIT
Thin windows were hard to fire into from the outside.
We could always just sit and wait until they run out of food and surrender. And I can't attack without a coffee.
When you just sit and wait, it's called a siege. Some sieges go on for months, even years. You're going to need a cookie with that . . .

Attack!

Mighty machines helped the enemy attack castle walls and the people inside. Even animals were used in the fight!

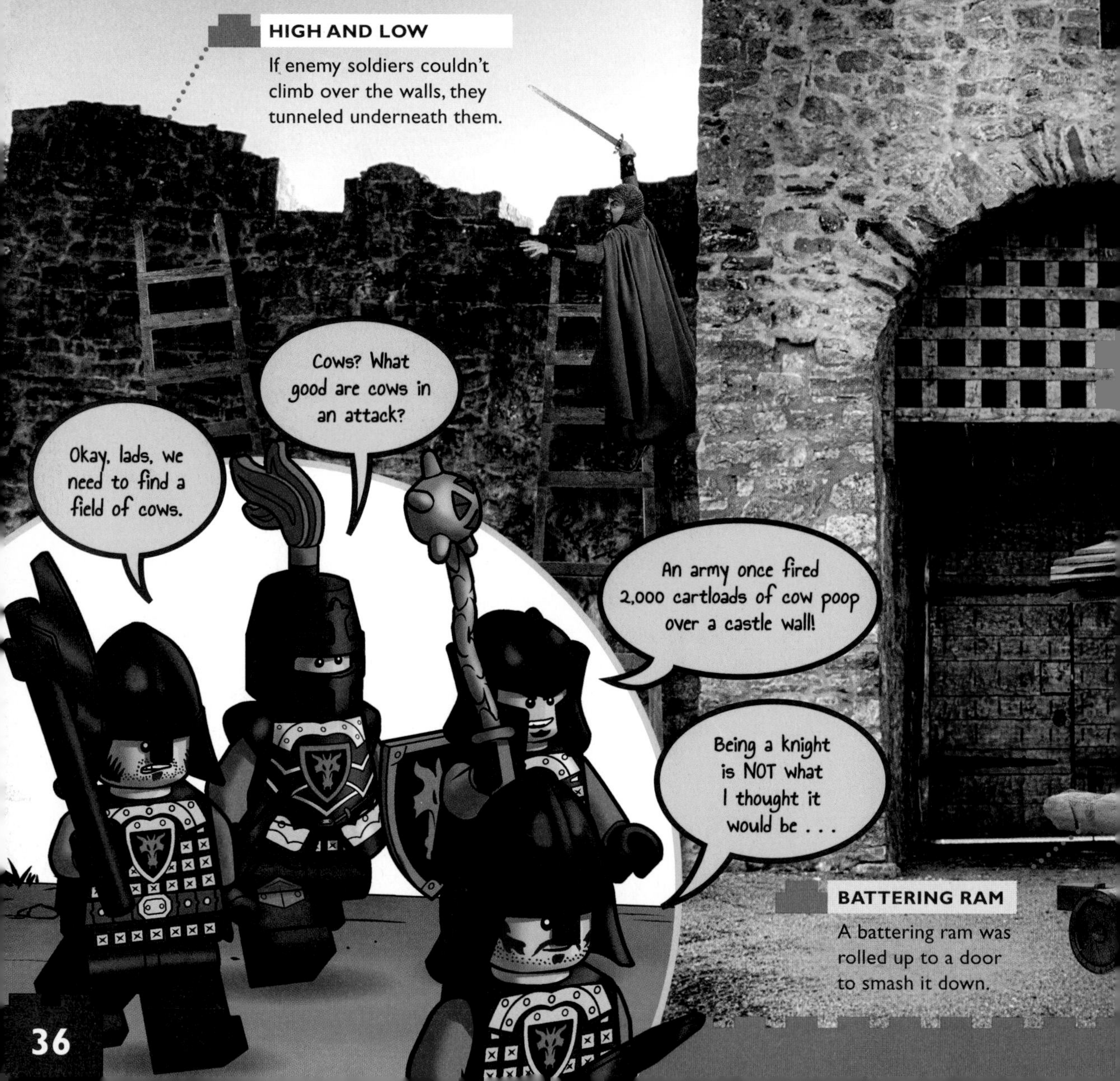
Cows? What good are cows in an attack?
Okay, lads, we need to find a field of cows.
An army once fired 2,000 cartloads of cow poop over a castle wall!
Being a knight is NOT what I thought it would be . . .

HIGH AND LOW

If enemy soldiers couldn't climb over the walls, they tunneled underneath them.

BATTERING RAM

A battering ram was rolled up to a door to smash it down.

Build it!
Build a giant belfry for your minifigures to jump off.

BELFRY

This machine was pushed against a wall so that men could climb up under cover.

As many as 2,000 stones could be hurled from a catapult in one day!

Oversize bows called ballistas shot giant arrows.

Beehives were fired into castles to cause crazy stinging.

Keep them out!

There was plenty that knights and soldiers could do to defend their castle. Attacks could go on for days or even weeks. The castle itself had some hidden tricks!

Hidden holes
Soldiers dropped everything they could on the enemy through holes at the tops of the walls.

ARCHERS
Medieval archers could fire an arrow about 200 feet (60 m).

Okay, lads! Bring out anything that we can drop ont our enemies' heads!

Stair trick
Staircases ran up clockwise. This made it easier for right-handed soldiers at the top of the stairs to fight enemies.

Portcullis
An iron gate called a portcullis could be lowered down in front of the castle door.

Birds were useful! Doves carried messages to other castles to ask for help.

Here's the dirty dishwater.
Sorry, I was asleep. I don't suppose my teddy is any good?
Huh?

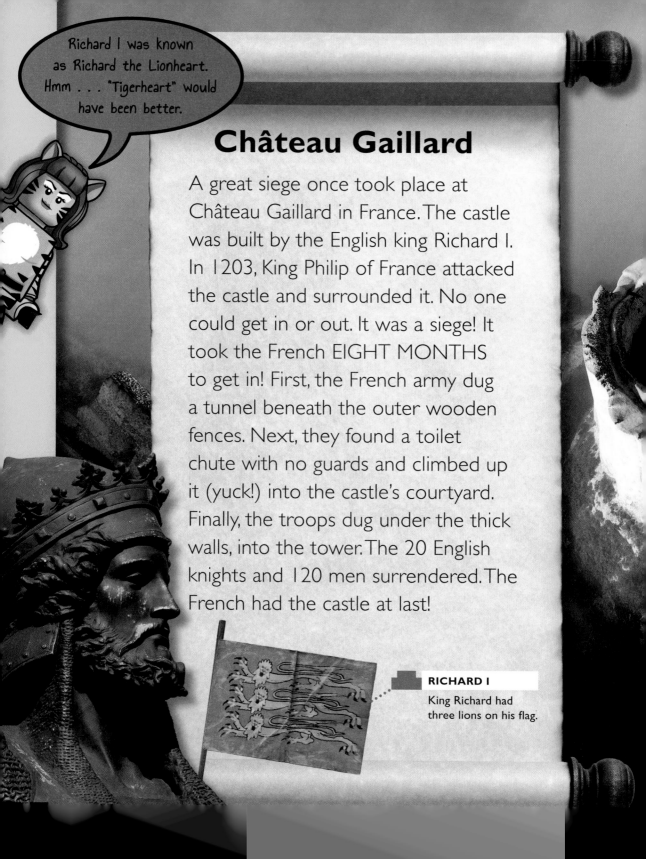

Richard I was known as Richard the Lionheart. Hmm . . . "Tigerheart" would have been better.

Château Gaillard

A great siege once took place at Château Gaillard in France. The castle was built by the English king Richard I. In 1203, King Philip of France attacked the castle and surrounded it. No one could get in or out. It was a siege! It took the French EIGHT MONTHS to get in! First, the French army dug a tunnel beneath the outer wooden fences. Next, they found a toilet chute with no guards and climbed up it (yuck!) into the castle's courtyard. Finally, the troops dug under the thick walls, into the tower. The 20 English knights and 120 men surrendered. The French had the castle at last!

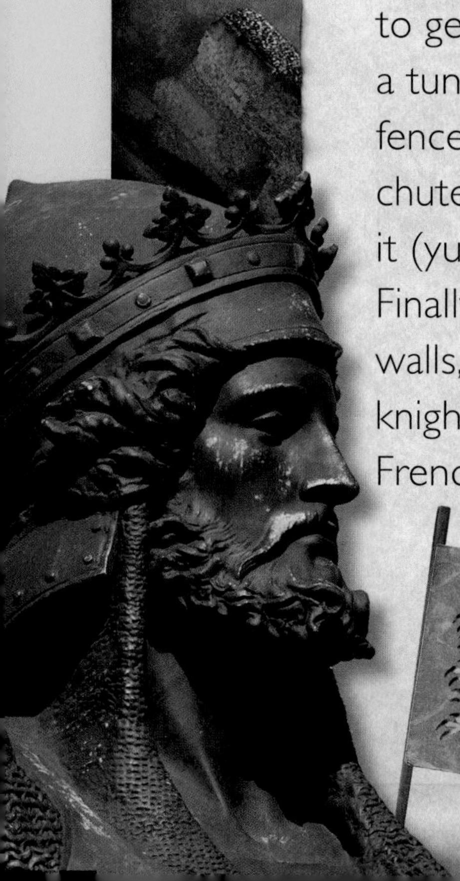

RICHARD I

King Richard had three lions on his flag.

We are under siege! Guard every door and tunnel, and keep your ears open.
Ahhh. A little peace and quiet. Time to relax . . .
Keep climbing, lads. Phew! This tunnel is stinky and really damp.
Whaaa—! Is there nowhere a knight can have a little time-out?!
Sometimes, when armies tunneled under walls, the soldiers inside would tunnel toward them and fight underground!

A knight's tale

EL CID

There are many statues of El Cid all over Spain, even though he lived almost 1,000 years ago!

PLAY IT!
Imagine the scariest knight ever! Now he can go into battle with your bravest knights.

El Cid, the most feared knight in Spain

In the 11th century, Rodrigo Diaz de Vivar, known as El Cid, was the most famous Spanish knight. Legend tells us that he defeated 300 of his enemies in one battle! El Cid first fought for Spain. But he upset a Spanish king, who banished him. El Cid then switched sides and won many battles with the enemy instead! When the Spanish king begged him to return, El Cid agreed. But he ended up making up his own army from both sides and taking a piece of Spain for himself. No one was going to rule El Cid!

El Cid has a pet lion. Don't panic, but it has escaped from its cage.
Aaarrrgh! Even that man's pets are scary. Tame it, will you?

Play it! Here are some ideas . . .

1. *What makes your knight so scary?*
2. *Does your hero have a terrifying pet?*
3. *What weapons does your knight use?*

Inside a castle

A castle was much more than just a fortress. It was a mini-town. Almost everything that the lord, lady, knights, and workers needed was inside the walls. Even animals were kept inside!

There weren't very many baths in a castle. The lord might have a soak in a wooden tub—but not often!
Is my bath ready? I haven't had one for a year!

Lord's room

The lord and lady had the only beds. Most people slept on wooden slats or on straw.

Bathroom

A castle did not have a toilet. Instead, there was a wooden seat with a hole. The waste dropped into a pit or moat.

Horses lived inside the castle walls, too!

Build it!
The lord needs a busy castle. Build the important things inside your castle walls. Here are some ideas.

Dungeon

Stables

Well

Gardens

Forge

Chapel

Kitchen
The kitchens were often far away from the lord's rooms and the great hall, in case they caught fire!

Well
There were no taps in a castle. Water was brought up from the ground through a well.

Build it bigger!
Sometimes an extra wall was built around the whole castle. Build another wall to keep your castle extra safe.

Who's who?

Castles were busy, crowded places. Everyone had a special job, and everyone was important. Here are some of the characters who lived in a castle.

No one can read this. Where's the chaplain?
Pay your money, please . . . or else. Grrrr.
Better pay your taxes, or you'll end up behind bars.

Chaplain
Many people were Christian. The chaplain was the castle's priest. Unlike most people, he could read and write.

Steward
The steward kept the servants in check and made sure that the serfs paid their taxes to the lord.

Constable
The constable was in charge of the guards and looked after the dungeon.

Build it!
The cook needs a kitchen to work in. Build one big enough to feed the whole castle!

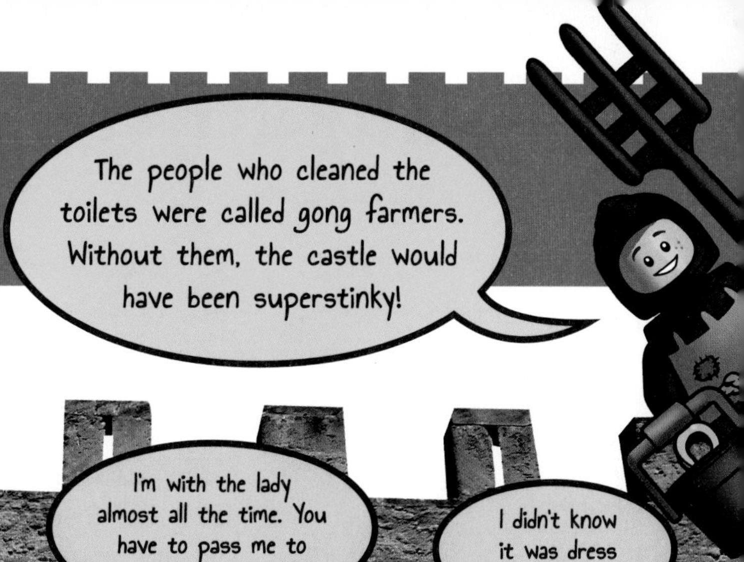
The people who cleaned the toilets were called gong farmers. Without them, the castle would have been superstinky!

I do dainty jobs, too. If the lord needs a necklace for his lady, I'm his man!
I'm with the lady almost all the time. You have to pass me to get to her!
I didn't know it was dress up day!

Blacksmith
The blacksmith's job was never-ending! He made horseshoes, nails, and tools, as well as weapons.

Lady-in-waiting
The lady-in-waiting helped the lady of the castle do all her daily tasks.

Cook
The cook had to make enough food for the whole castle. He also cooked huge feasts for festivals.

A day in the castle

As soon as the bell rings, everyone gets up to start a busy day of hard work in the castle!

4:00 AM: Get up!
The bell rings as early as 4:00 AM! The servants have lit the fires. The lord and lady get up and have their breakfast.

6:00 AM: Work time!
The market stalls open in the courtyard. Everyone starts a busy day of work. At 8:00 AM, the castle gates open.

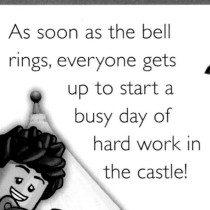

With no electricity to light up their houses, people got up at sunrise and went to bed at sunset.

NO ONE is allowed out at night. Not even for some fresh air.

10:00 AM: Lunch
Lunch is the main meal of the day—at 10:00 AM! The lord and lady often have six courses! Supper is eaten at 3:00 PM.

7:00 PM: Curfew
A bell is rung for curfew. This means that all the people in the castle have to go inside their houses, and the castle gates are shut.

Night watchman
A soldier patrols the castle at night to make sure that everyone stays inside. He watches for enemies, too.

EWERER

The ewerer brought and heated water for the lord and lady. It was a busy job!

Only rich kids went to school. We just learned to do the jobs that our parents did.
It's all right for you—your dad was a blacksmith. Mine was a gong farmer. Phew!

Don't do it!

KNIGHT FACTS
Knights taken prisoner in battle could be thrown into the dungeon. It was possible to pay to release them.

Don't break the law in the castle! One of the worst thing that anyone could do was steal. A thief would be thrown into a dark dungeon or made to stand in the pillory!

Pillory

A thief's hands and head were locked into a wooden plank, called a pillory, that was kept in the castle courtyard. Then people threw rotten fruit and vegetables at the thief!

TICKLE TORTURE

Sometimes a thief's feet would be locked into stocks, and goats would lick them!

I sentence you to the goat and rotten veggies.
NO! NOT THE GOAT! I'm too ticklish!

Build it!

Build a castle dungeon that no one can escape from!

Dark and dim

Most dungeons were cold, dark rooms, no bigger than most bathrooms. About 10 to 20 prisoners were kept there at a time.

BEHIND BARS

A thief was lucky to get a window to look out of.

RATS

Dungeons were freezing cold and were often filled with rats!

Woo-hoo! I've got lots of stinking vegetables to get rid of.
Throw the cabbage. It can't be worse than prison food.

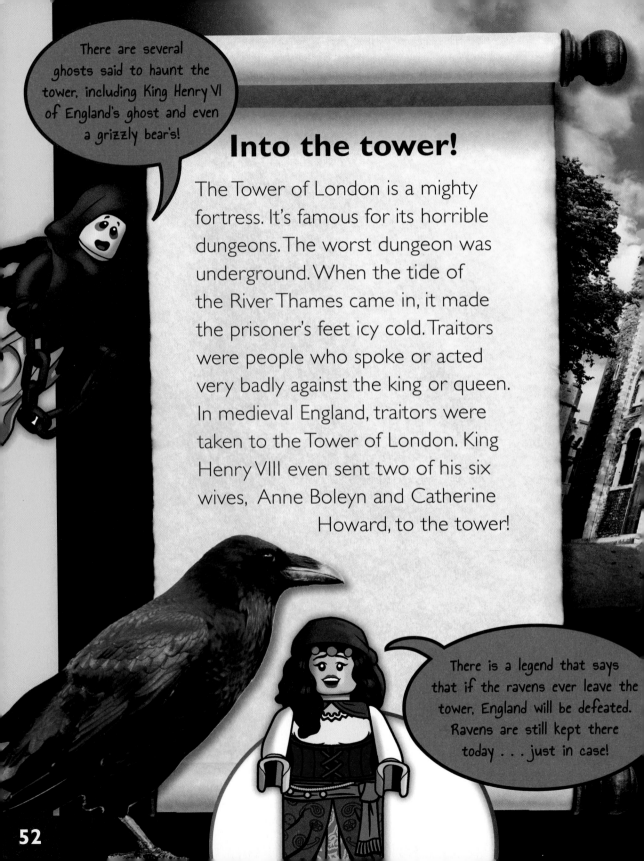

There are several ghosts said to haunt the tower, including King Henry VI of England's ghost and even a grizzly bear's!

Into the tower!

The Tower of London is a mighty fortress. It's famous for its horrible dungeons. The worst dungeon was underground. When the tide of the River Thames came in, it made the prisoner's feet icy cold. Traitors were people who spoke or acted very badly against the king or queen. In medieval England, traitors were taken to the Tower of London. King Henry VIII even sent two of his six wives, Anne Boleyn and Catherine Howard, to the tower!

There is a legend that says that if the ravens ever leave the tower, England will be defeated. Ravens are still kept there today . . . just in case!

ELEPHANT TOWER

The Tower of London was also a zoo. In the early 1200s, an elephant was kept in a tower!

Anne Boleyn

I do NOT like the king's new crown.
Phew! The king has stinky breath!
I can see the king's underpants!
Here's what NOT to say to the king.

Pet birds of prey

All kinds of animals were castle pets. Falcons were very popular birds in medieval times. Every lord had one. They were trained to hunt and then fly back to their owners. Trained falcons were worth more than their weight in gold.

THE HUNT

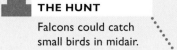

Falcons could catch small birds in midair.

Falcon training

Falcons were trained by falconers to catch small mammals and birds. It took years to train a falcon, so only rich people owned one.

If you steal a falcon, the punishment is to let it peck you—ouch!
Good thing I'm made of straw.

LET'S PARTY!

Lords threw huge parties to show off their falcons.

Build it!
Build a big bird of prey. Make sure that it has huge wings!

FALCON

Falcons were the most popular birds to train. But hawks and eagles were used, too.

HOOD

A hood kept the falcon calm. Hoods were often decorated with jewels.

BELLS

Bells on the falcon's feet helped the owner hear where it was in the sky.

A great feast

In medieval times, everyone loved a feast. The biggest castle room, the great hall, was decorated. Entertainers sang and danced. Let the feast begin!

The high table

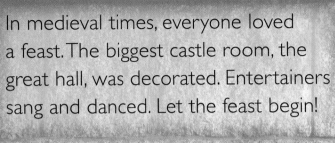

The lord and lady sat at the high table, a table on a platform. Even today, people have "high tables" at parties for important guests.

Fancy foods

In addition to deer and wild boar, foods such as swan, heron, and peacock were cooked on huge fires and served with bread.

FINGER FOOD

There were no forks. People ate with knives and their fingers!

Medieval table manners

Sorry . . . ACHOOOO!

DON'T blow your nose on your napkin.

Did you want me to cut your swan, my lord?

DON'T clean your nails with your eating knife.

Mmm, almost done!

DON'T pick up your bowl and lick it.

BUURRP!

DON'T burp in someone's face.

This . . . is . . . yummy.

DON'T spit on the table (just on the floor).

I'm very gentle, you know. Wouldn't hurt a flea.

DON'T scratch the fleas on your head.

This knight had bad table manners!

MORE ALE!

Ale and wine were drunk in medieval times.

MEDIEVAL JESTER

Jesters dressed to look funny. They often wore hats that looked like donkeys' ears. The stick with the head on it was called a bauble.

PLAY IT!
Perhaps it is time for a great feast in your castle. Where is the jester?

was so good, the king gave him a huge house!

Every castle had its own jester. The jester's job was to entertain the household. Jesters sang, played music, told stories and jokes, juggled, and did magic. They were often acrobats, too! In the 12th century, there lived a jester named Roland. He was jester to King Henry II of England. He was so good at his job that the king gave him a manor house. All Roland had to do was perform one jump, one whistle, and one fart, once a year, every Christmas!

I need cheering up. What can you come up with?
HEY, JESTER! You know you have to be ready, day or night, to entertain the king.
Hold on, Your Majesty. I think I'm getting my second wind . . .
. . . PARP!

Play it! Here are some ideas . . .

1 *Does your jester have a silly name?*

2 *Does he have a special talent?*

3 *Perhaps the jester secretly wants to be a knight.*

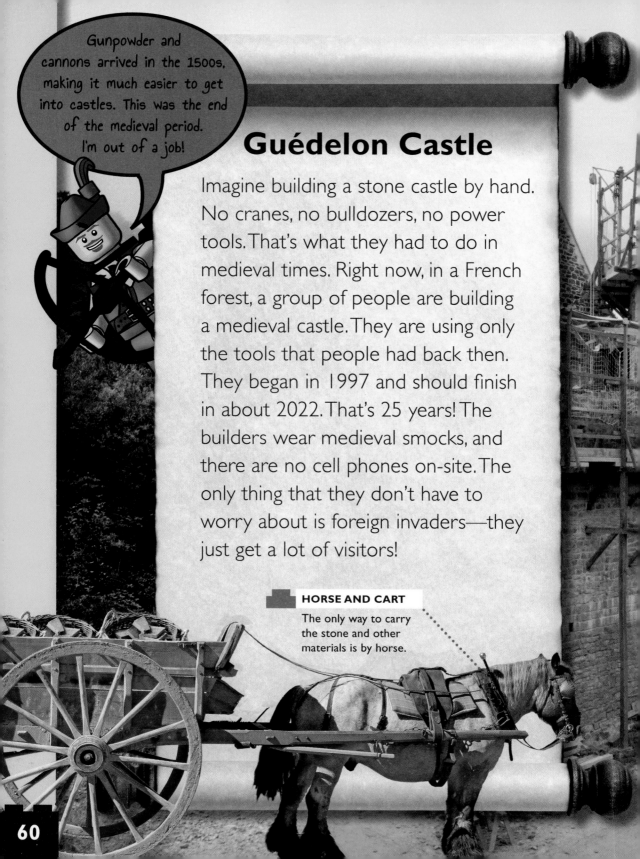

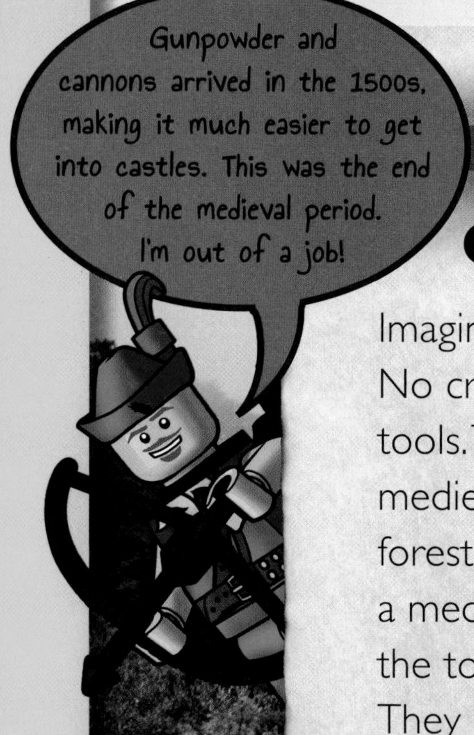
Gunpowder and cannons arrived in the 1500s, making it much easier to get into castles. This was the end of the medieval period. I'm out of a job!

Guédelon Castle

Imagine building a stone castle by hand. No cranes, no bulldozers, no power tools. That's what they had to do in medieval times. Right now, in a French forest, a group of people are building a medieval castle. They are using only the tools that people had back then. They began in 1997 and should finish in about 2022. That's 25 years! The builders wear medieval smocks, and there are no cell phones on-site. The only thing that they don't have to worry about is foreign invaders—they just get a lot of visitors!

HORSE AND CART

The only way to carry the stone and other materials is by horse.

Let's dress up and build a castle!
You know, it took about 12 years to build a large castle in medieval times.
Bring in the power! We'll finish the job in a year!
Beat it, buddy! This is a power-tool-free zone.
No toilets or taps! This job will be easy!

Glossary

arena
An enclosed place used for entertainment.

battlement
A low wall at the top of a castle or a tower with open spaces to shoot through.

blacksmith
A worker who shapes iron by heating and hammering it in order to make weapons, horseshoes, etc.

curfew
A law that tells people to be off the streets at a certain time at night.

chivalry
The ways in which a knight should act to be good and well-behaved.

dungeon
A dark, usually underground, prison.

fortress
A large walled place that often has a town inside it.

jester
A joker, or clown, who entertains guests and makes them laugh.

herald
A person who brings news or carries messages.

legend
A story from the past that people believe to be true, but no one can be certain that it is.

minstrel
A person who sings and tells stories to people.

motto
A short group of words that tells a person or group how they should try to live or behave.

Did you say that the Château Gaillard seige lasted eight months? We are definitely going to need more coffee . . .

order
A special club that knights belong to who follow the same rules.

page
A youth being trained for knighthood who works for a knight.

siege
When an army surrounds a fortress or city to force it to give itself up, or surrender.

smock
A loose shirt usually worn over clothes to protect them from dirt.

squire
A young man who carries the shield or armor of a knight, until he becomes a knight himself.

subject
A person who is stands by, and fights for, a king or queen.

tapestry
A heavy cloth that has pictures woven into it. It is often hung on a wall.

tournament
A contest of skill between knights wearing armor and fighting with blunted lances or swords.

World castles
Since medieval times, lots of different-shaped castles have been built all over the world.

Eilean Donan Castle, Scotland

Malbork Castle, Poland

Qasr al-Kharanah, Jordan

Neuschwanstein Castle, Germany

Himeji Castle, Japan

Sleeping Beauty Castle, Disneyland

Build it!
Design your own castle in the best shape ever! You could use some of the shapes in the pictures above, or you could invent your own. Happy castle building!

Index and credits

Index

Credits

For the LEGO Group: Randi Kirsten Sørensen *Assistant Manager*; Peter Moorby *Licensing Coordinator*; Heidi K. Jensen *Licensing Manager*; Paul Hansford *Creative Publishing Manager*; Martin Leighton Lindhardt *Publishing Graphic Designer*
Photographs ©: cover crown: jgroup/iStockphoto; cover explosions: magann/Fotolia; cover castle: Patryk Kosmider/Shutterstock, Inc.; back cover top left: Fulcanelli/Shutterstock, Inc.; back cover bottom left: Rob Hainer/Shutterstock, Inc.; back cover bottom right: Nejron/Dreamstime; 1 background: Fabio Pagani/Shutterstock, Inc.; 1 knight: JochenK/iStockphoto; 2 bottom left: Natalia Catalina/Shutterstock, Inc.; 2 bottom left rat and throughout: wildcat78/iStockphoto; 2 bottom right rat and throughout: Antagain/iStockphoto; 2 center right: DanielBendjy/iStockphoto; 4 top left shield and throughout: Andrey Kuzmin/iStockphoto; 4-5 top background: Fabio Pagani/Shutterstock, Inc.; 5 center left knight: JochenK/iStockphoto; 6 left castle: mmr2008/Fotolia; 6 bottom left fence: Anest/iStockphoto; 6 right castle: esinel_888/Fotolia; 6-7 sky background: IP Galanternik D.U./iStockphoto; 6-7 green hills: barrand/iStockphoto; 6-7 stone wall: Bennewitz/iStockphoto; 7 center castle: Rolf E. Staerk/Shutterstock, Inc.; 7 right top left: RFStock/iStockphoto; 7 right top right: ifish/iStockphoto; 7 right center left: GgWink/iStockphoto; 7 right center right: CaronB/iStockphoto; 7 right bottom left: Sophonibal/iStockphoto; 7 right bottom right: plrang/iStockphoto; 8 bottom left: Mlenny/iStockphoto; 8 bottom right: Studio-Annika/iStockphoto; 8-9 stone wall background: Atlaspix/Shutterstock, Inc.; 8-9 sky background: IP Galanternik D.U./iStockphoto; 9 bottom left: sadman0026/iStockphoto; 9 bottom center: Vladimirs_Gorelovs/iStockphoto; 9 bottom right chickens: yands/iStockphoto; 9 bottom right eggs: Pauws99/iStockphoto; 9 top castle and hill: sueburtonphotography/Dreamstime; 10 center left: Leah-Anne Thompson/Shutterstock, Inc.; 10 center right: Gordana Sermek/Shutterstock, Inc.; 10-11 background: optimarc/Shutterstock, Inc.; 11 center left: Grisha Bruev/Shutterstock, Inc.; 11 right: propositive/Shutterstock, Inc.; 11 top left: fotofrankyat/iStockphoto; 12 center left: DianaHirsch/iStockphoto; 12 bottom left: ranasu/iStockphoto; 12-13 top background: Ken Rygh/iStockphoto; 12-13 tile floor : NUMAX3D/iStockphoto; 12-13 knights: Nejron Photo/Shutterstock, Inc.; 13 scroll: ajaykampani/iStockphoto; 13 bottom right: galdzer/iStockphoto; 14-15 background: Vladimir Wrangel/Shutterstock, Inc.; 16 center: acceptfoto/iStockphoto; 16-17 aged paper background and throughout: Peter Zelei/iStockphoto; 17 quill and throughout: kutaytanir/iStockphoto; 17 ink spots and throughout: mashabr/iStockphoto; 18 knight: Sylphe_7/iStockphoto; 18-19 tile floor: NUMAX3D/iStockphoto; 19 top right: Atmosphere1/Shutterstock, Inc.; 19 bottom right: Natalia Catalina/Shutterstock, Inc.; 20 background, 21: Attila445/iStockphoto; 22 center: mitza/iStockphoto; 24 shield: Tim Loughhead/Precision Illustration; 24-25 bottom background: puchan/iStockphoto; 25 top left: flowersandclassicalmusic/iStockphoto; 25 top right coats of arms: Zdenek Harnoch/Shutterstock, Inc.; 26 center: World History Archive/Alamy Images; 26 bottom left scroll: zoom-zoom/iStockphoto; 26 bottom left: The Art Archive/Alamy Images; 27 bottom left: danielsbfoto/iStockphoto; 27 center: World History Archive/Alamy Images; 28 right knight: Géher/Fotolia; 28-29 top background: PLRANG ART/Shutterstock, Inc.; 29 center left stick: Miriam2009/iStockphoto; 29 center left flag: duncan1890/iStockphoto; 29 top: INTERFOTO/Alamy Images; 30 center: imageBROKER/Alamy Images; 32 scroll and throughout: Lisa Thornberg/iStockphoto; 32-33 background: Romeo Huidu/Shutterstock, Inc.; 34, 35 background: TimothyBall/iStockphoto; 36 ladders: Aptyp_koK/iStockphoto; 36 center knight: jpique/iStockphoto; 36-37 background: Patryk Kosmider/Shutterstock, Inc.; 37 top right: Oleg Znamenskiy/Shutterstock, Inc.; 37 center right: mtcurado/iStockphoto; 37 center tower: grafvision/Shutterstock, Inc.; 37 bottom left : Aleksei Lazukov/iStockphoto; 37 bottom center man: Jaroslaw Grudzinski/Shutterstock, Inc.; 38 top archer: agno_agnus/Fotolia; 38 bottom archer: Andrea Rizzotti/Fotolia; 38 top right: Nick Hawkes/Shutterstock, Inc.; 38-39 background: mylisa/Fotolia; 39 top center: Andrey_Kuzmin/Shutterstock, Inc.; 39 right bow and arrow: Farmer/Fotolia; 39 top left: mtreasure/iStockphoto; 40 bottom left: RFStock/iStockphoto; 40 bottom center stick: Miriam2009/iStockphoto; 40 bottom center flag: duncan1890/iStockphoto; 40-41 background: Hemis/Alamy Images; 42 center: BotondHorvath/iStockphoto; 44 bottom left tub: Mauro69/iStockphoto; 44 bottom left rubber duck: Turnervisual/iStockphoto; 44 bottom left bubbles: Floortje/iStockphoto; 44 bottom left foam: Dmytro_Skorobogatov/iStockphoto; 44 bottom center: Patryk Kosmider/Shutterstock, Inc.; 44 bottom right: villorejo/iStockphoto; 44-45 background: Ammit Jack/Shutterstock, Inc.; 45 horse: rusm/iStockphoto; 45 bottom left: fotorince/Fotolia; 45 bottom center: snem/iStockphoto; 45 right top left: Pack-Shot/iStockphoto; 45 right top right: vicuschka/iStockphoto; 45 right center left: snem/iStockphoto; 45 right center right: kodachrome25/iStockphoto; 45 right bottom left: Philartphace/iStockphoto; 45 right bottom right: kisstochka15/iStockphoto; 46 bottom left: Studio-Annika/iStockphoto; 46 bottom center top: Thomas Demarczyk/iStockphoto; 46 bottom center bottom: Elna_Ozornina/iStockphoto; 46 bottom right top: spuno/Fotolia; 46 bottom right bottom: BlackAperture/iStockphoto; 46-47 stone wall background: Atlaspix/Shutterstock, Inc.; 47 bottom left: eddy02/iStockphoto; 47 bottom center: Petrafler/Shutterstock, Inc.; 47 bottom right top: shaunwilkinson/Fotolia; 47 bottom right bottom: johny007pan/iStockphoto; 48 top center bell: sarikosta/Shutterstock, Inc.; 48 top center: Patryk Kosmider/Shutterstock, Inc.; 48 center left tent: artemrybchak/Shutterstock, Inc.; 48 bottom background: leskas/iStockphoto; 48 bottom right: Razvan/iStockphoto; 48 top right: Razvan/iStockphoto; 48-49 stone wall background: Atlaspix/Shutterstock, Inc.; 49 top left: zee2000/iStockphoto; 49 top center: Wibofoto/iStockphoto; 49 bottom background: Michal Krakowiak/iStockphoto; 49 center right: ermingut/iStockphoto; 49 bottom right: Razvan/iStockphoto; 50 bottom left cabbage: olya6105/Fotolia; 50 bottom apples: pingu2004/Fotolia; 50 bottom right cabbage: wilddrago/Fotolia; 50 bottom turnip and carrot: superfood/Fotolia; 50 bottom beet: efebvre_jonathan/Fotolia; 50 bottom tomato: efebvre_jonathan/Fotolia; 50 center right stocks: Aigars Reinholds/Shutterstock, Inc.; 50 bottom left ball and chain: Asmus Koefoed/Shutterstock, Inc.; 50 center left goat: ollirg/Shutterstock, Inc.; 50-51 squashed tomatoes: Picsfive/Shutterstock, Inc.; 50-51 bottom background: optimarc/Shutterstock, Inc.; 51 bottom right: Asmus Koefoed/Shutterstock, Inc.; 51 right: Tamara Kulikova/Shutterstock, Inc.; 51 top left: PRILL/Shutterstock, Inc.; 52 bottom left: purplevine/iStockphoto; 52-53 background: mtrommer/iStockphoto; 53 bottom left: duncan1890/iStockphoto; 54 top right birds: Andyworks/iStockphoto; 54-55 background: Bikeworldtravel/Shutterstock, Inc.; 55 falcon: Elle1/Shutterstock, Inc.; 56 top right: ajafoto/iStockphoto; 56 center left queen: Yuri_Arcurs/iStockphoto; 56 center right king and food: Yuri_Arcurs/iStockphoto; 56 center right bottle: ihoe/iStockphoto; 56-57 background: optimarc/Shutterstock, Inc.; 56-57 table: Piotr Krzeslak/iStockphoto; 57 scroll: ajaykampani/iStockphoto; 57 bottom left candle: VeraPetruk/iStockphoto; 57 right: Kachalkina Veronika/Shutterstock, Inc.; 58 center: Chris Hellier/Alamy Images; 60 bottom left cart: amandine45/iStockphoto; 60 bottom left tiles: Rrrainbow/iStockphoto; 60 left background: MarioGuti/iStockphoto; 60 right background, 61 background: Jaime Pharr/Shutterstock, Inc.; 61 bottom left: Huang Zheng/Shutterstock, Inc.; 62 castle: esinel_888/Fotolia; 62-63 top background: barrand/iStockphoto; 63 right top left: Maciej Noskowski/iStockphoto; 63 right top right: ewg3D/iStockphoto; 63 right center right: bluejayphoto/iStockphoto; 63 right bottom left: hayakato/iStockphoto; 63 right bottom right: Pavel L Photo and Video/Shutterstock, Inc.; 63 right center left: JPRichard/Shutterstock, Inc.; 64 top: Andrey_Kuzmin/Shutterstock, Inc.

All LEGO® illustrations by Paul Lee.

In 1500, medieval times ended. I'm off!